Fetish Fashion

KÖNEMANN

Fetish Fashion

ARDITA FETISH FASHION 6
COLLECTIVE CHAOS 28
LUCKY DAME 46
WESTWARD BOUND 56
ROSE CONWAY PHOTOGRAPHY 80
HEVEAS HEAVEN 98
INNER SANCTUM 106
MAEBELLE LATEX 120
LOVELY LATEX 128
DOS SANTOS 138
EUSTRATIA 150
CYBERESQUE 164
BLACKLICKORISH LATEX 178
GODFREY KNIGHT DESIGNS 194
AINSLEY - T SHOES 200
GORE COUTURE CORSETRY 212
MISS OVERDOSE 222
ROYALBLACK 230
LENA QUIST 240
TWOTWENTYTWO CLOTHING 254
ELECTRIC IBIZA 266
FEISTY CAT 270

SHHH! COUTURE 286
TATJANA WARNECKE COSMIC COUTURE BERLIN 298
AM STATIK 314
LIBIDEX LTD 328
FAVOR 344
RALF FRANZ FOTODESIGN 356
HW DESIGN 364
SENSUAL LATEX 372
FABULOUSLY LATEX 388
DONALD PILON 400
ARCANUM ACCESSORIES 404
CATHOUSE CLOTHING 414
ZITRONENRÖLLCHEN 424
KIMBERLICIOUS LATEX 436
MAD DUCK DESIGNS 446
VALERIA ORLANDO 462
TABLEAUX VIVANTS 466
PHOTO CREDITS 478

When asked about the difference between art and sexuality, Picasso replied: "They are one and the same, because art is always erotic."

(Picasso)

Interrogé sur la différence entre l'art et la sexualité, Picasso avait répondu : « Il s'agit d'une seule et même chose, car l'art est toujours érotiqu. »

(Picasso)

Gefragt nach dem Unterschied zwischen Kunst und Sexualität, antwortete Picasso: „Es handelt sich um ein und dasselbe, denn Kunst ist immer erotisch."

(Picasso)

Op de vraag naar het verschil tussen kunst en seksualiteit antwoordde Picasso: "Het is een en hetzelfde, want kunst is altijd erotisch."

(Picasso)

Preguntado por la diferencia entre el arte y la sexualidad, Picasso respondía: "Son lo mismo, ya que el arte es siempre erótico."

(Picasso)

Alla domanda, qual è la differenza tra arte e sessualità, Picasso risponde: "Si tratta sempre della stessa cosa, perché l'arte è sempre erotica."

(Picasso)

Quando perguntaram a Picasso qual era a diferença entre arte e sexualidade, este respondeu: "São uma e a mesma coisa, pois a arte é sempre erótica."

(Picasso)

När Picasso fick frågan om skillnaden mellan konst och sexualitet svarade han: "Det handlar om samma sak. Konsten är alltid erotisk."

(Picasso)

ARDITA
FETISH FASHION

Model: Ophelia Overdose

Model: Ophelia Overdose

Model: Ophelia Overdose

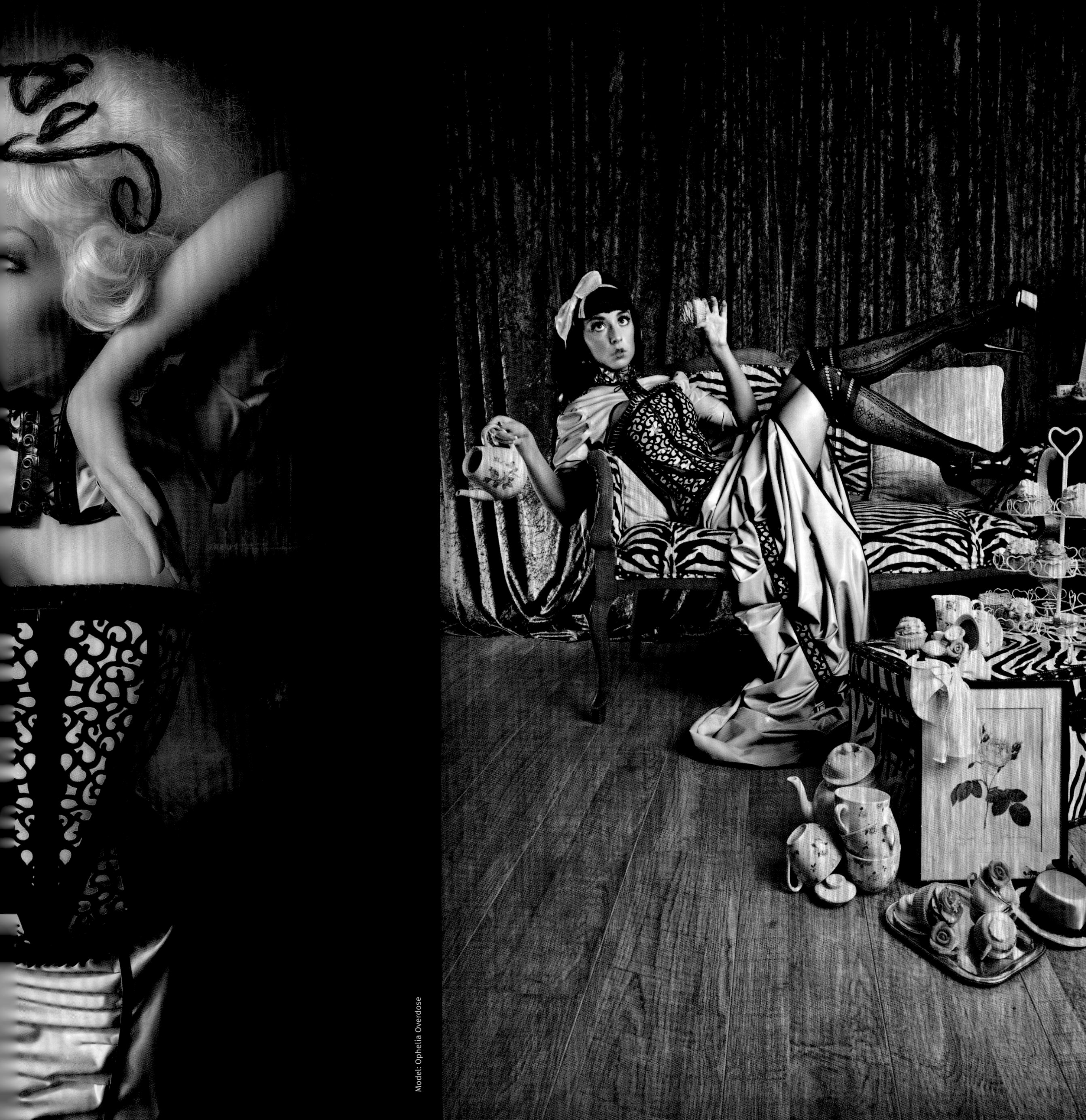

Model: Ophelia Overdose

Geschiedenis van het
VLIEGEN
HELMUT NEWTON
GRISHAM
ARAFAT
DAVID LACHAPELLE HEAVEN TO HELL
ATLAS OF THE WORLD
MOEDERS

Ardita Fetish Fashion

COLLECTIVE CHAOS

WELCOME

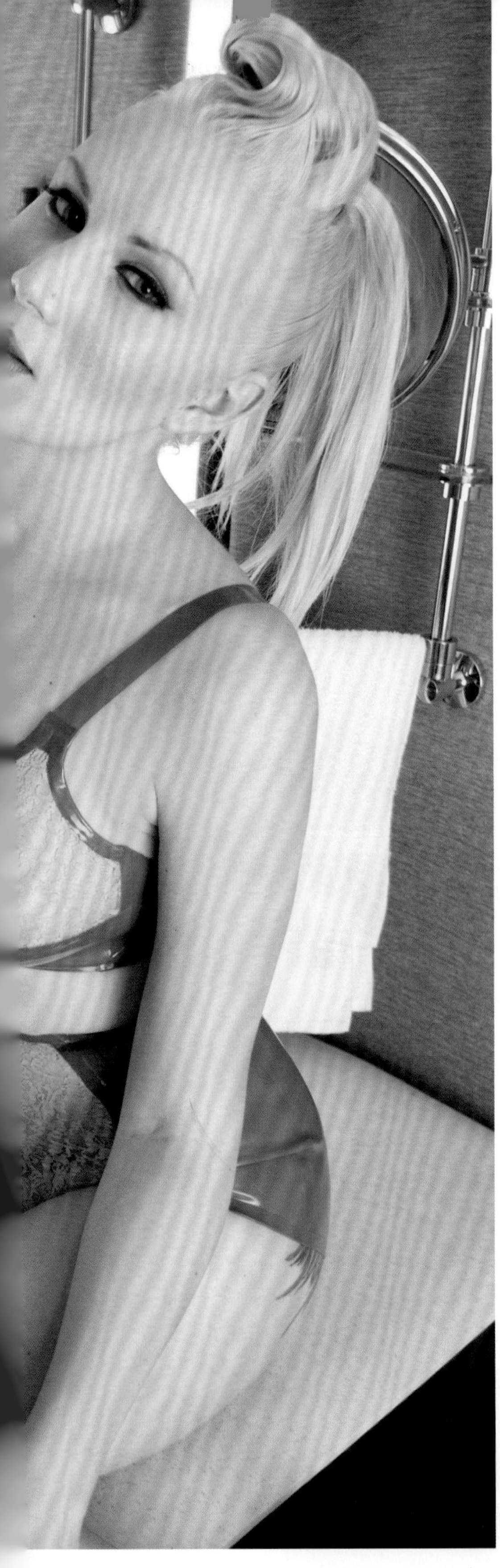

Collective Chaos

LUCKY DAME

LOADSTAR

Lucky Dame

WESTWARD BOUND

Model: Ophelia Overdose

Model: Ophelia Overdose

Model: Ophelia Overdose

Model: Ophelia Overdose

Model: Ophelia Overdose

Model: Ophelia Overdose

Model: Ophelia Overdose

Model: Ophelia Overdose

FLOHR-OTIS
47NF1421 1974
2
1
E
K
TELEFON
1100 Kg
TRAGFÄHIGKEIT
16 PERSONEN
ODER
VON DER SCHACHTWAND ZURÜCKTRETEN

Model: Ophelia Overdose

Model: Ophelia Overdose

Model: Ophelia Overdose

Westward Bound

ROSE CONWAY PHOTOGRAPHY

vincit

Rose Conway Photography

HEVEAS HEAVEN

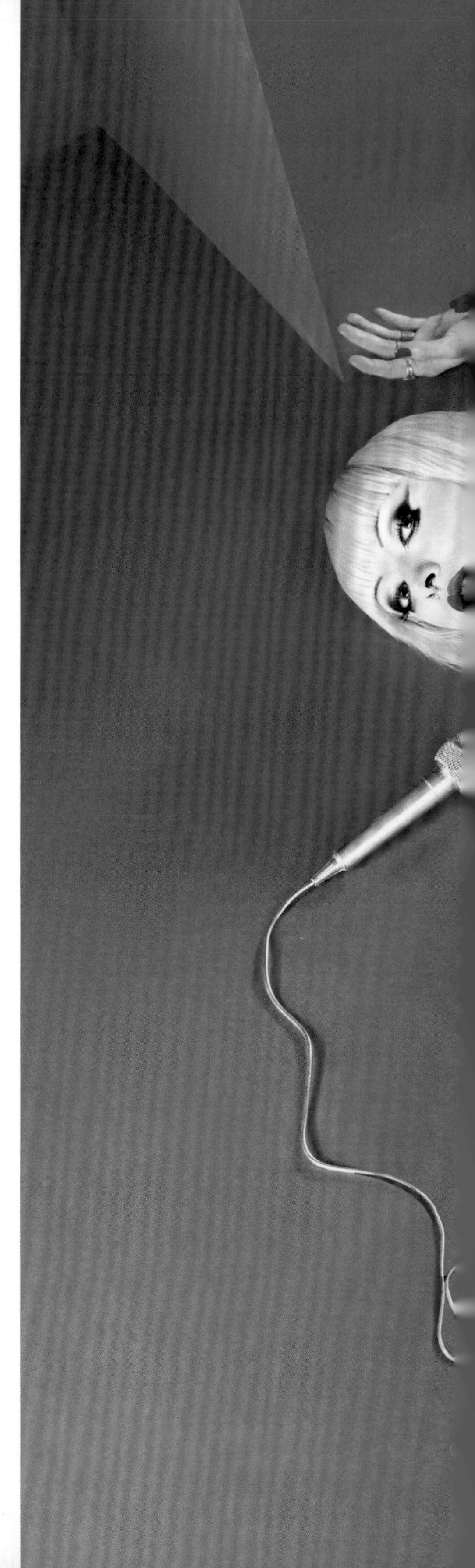

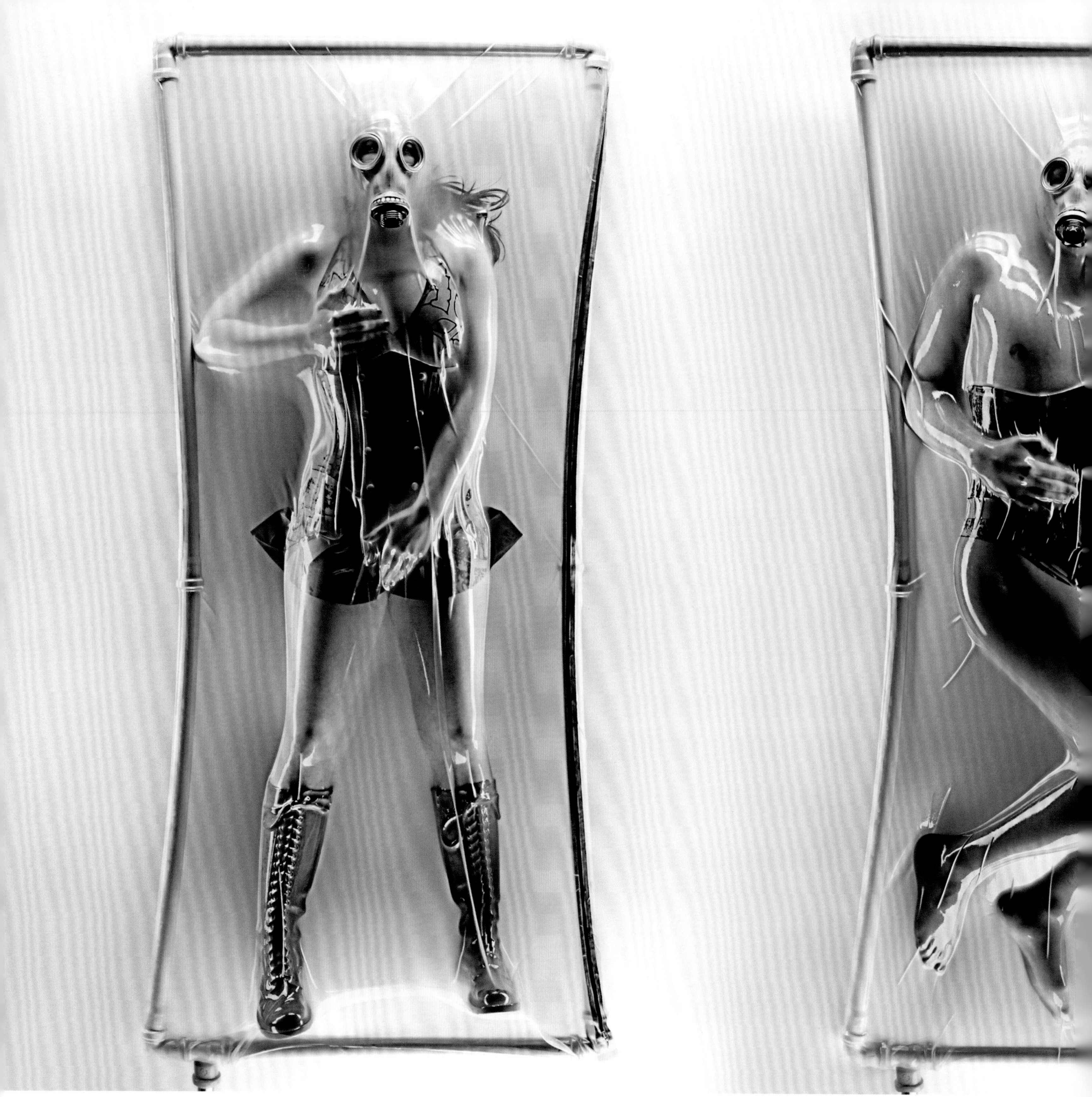

Heveas Heaven

INNER SANCTUM

Inner Sanctum

SANCTUM
INNER SANCTUM
INNER SANCTUM
INNER SANCTUM

inner sanctum
inner sanctum
inner sanctum
inner

INNER SANCTUM
INNER SANCTUM
INNER SANCTUM

Inner Sanctum Showroom

MAEBELLE LATEX

Maebelle Latex

LOVELY LATEX

Model: Ophelia Overdose

Model: Ophelia Overdose

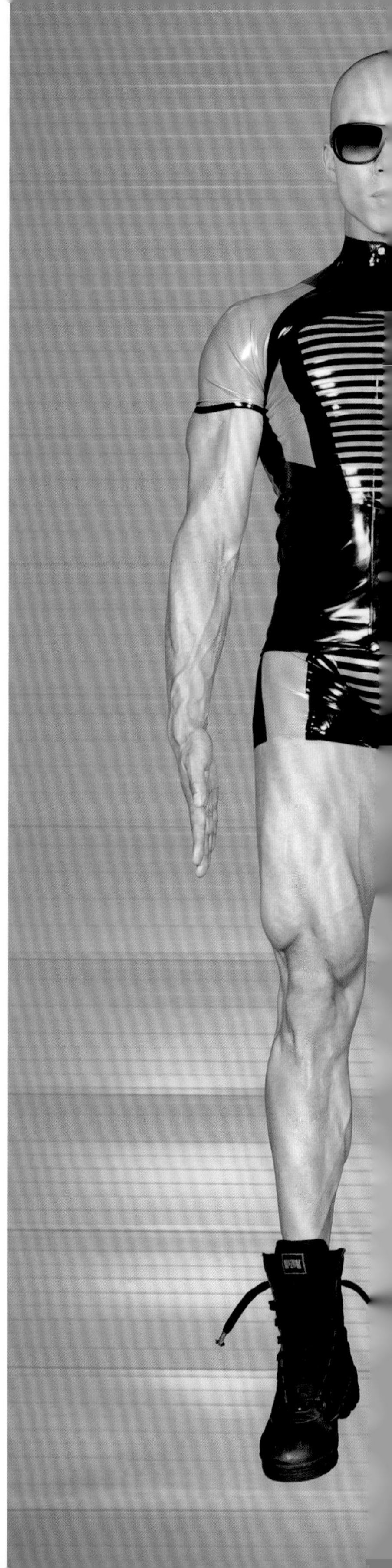

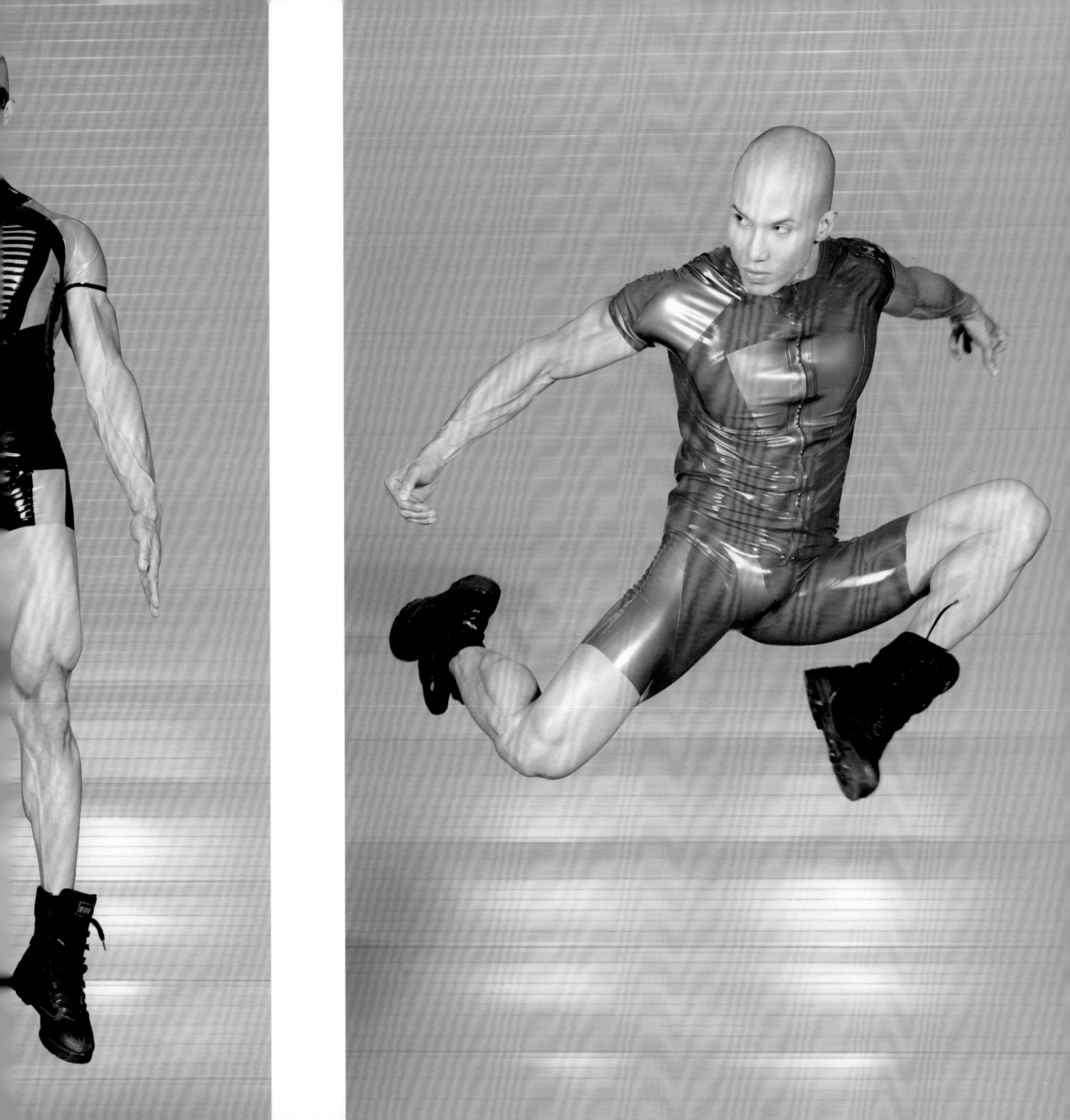

Lovely Latex

DOS SANTOS

dos santos

EUSTRATIA

Eustratia

Eustratia

MODEL: OPHELIA OVERDOSE

Leer
UV

Cyberesque

BLACKLICKORISH LATEX

Blacklickorish Latex

GODFREY KNIGHT DESIGNS

Godfrey Knight Designs

AINSLEY - T SHOES

FUCK ME

FUCK ME

ainsley-t shoes

GORE COUTURE CORSETRY

Core Couture Corsetry & Creations by Liv Free

Core Couture Corsetry & Creations by Liv Free

Gore Couture Corsetry

Corset design: Photo by Moritz Maibaum, Model: Ophelia Overdose

MISS OVERDOSE

Corset design: Photo by Marcus Gunnarsson, Models: Elegy Ellem & Ophelia Overdose

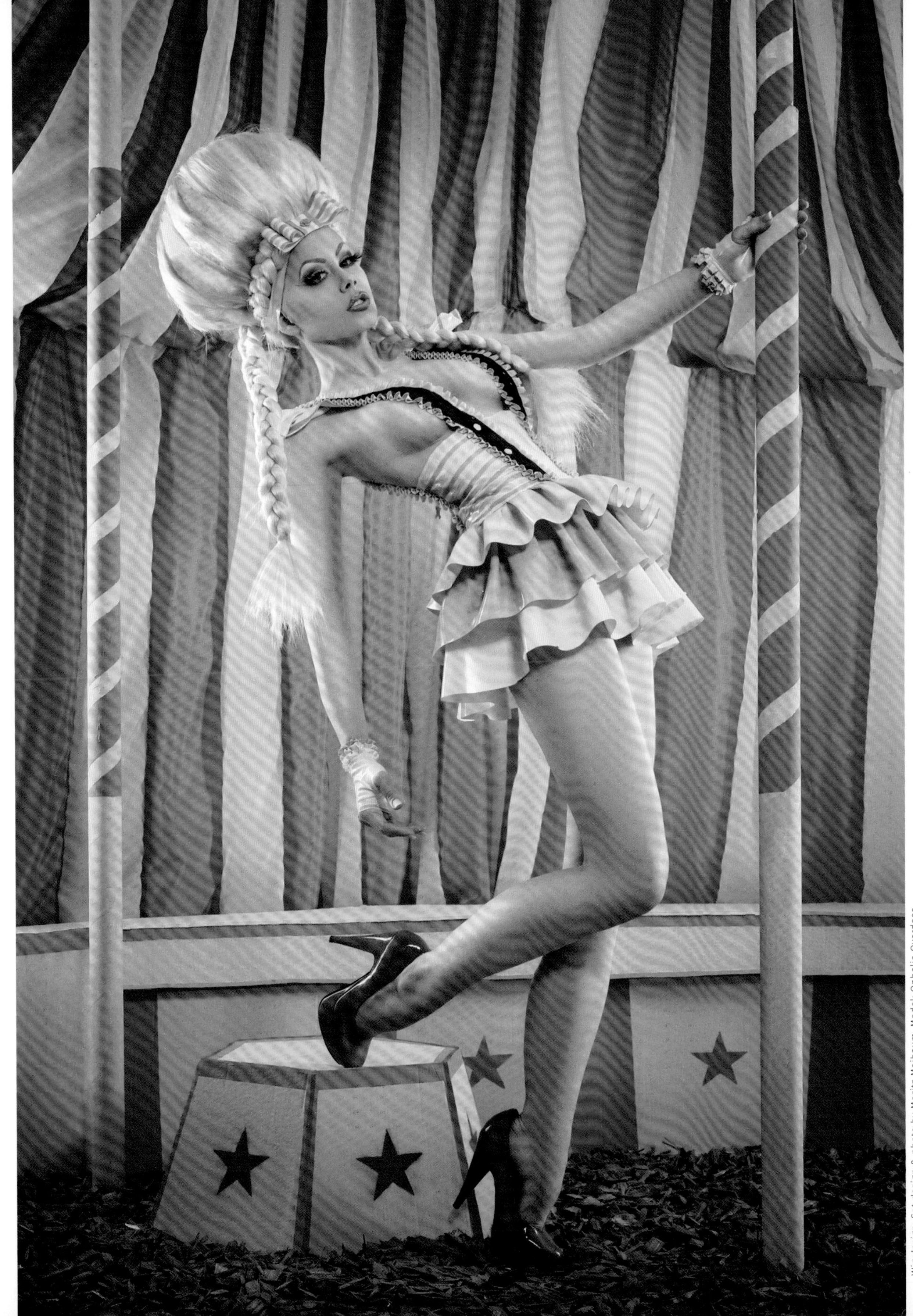

Wig design: Set design & photo by Moritz Maibaum, Model: Ophelia Overdose

Wig design: Set design & photo by Moritz Maibaum, Model: Ophelia Overdose

Headgear: Photo by Hartmut Norenberg, Model: Ophelia Overdose

Latex costume: Photo by Hartmut Norenberg, Model: Ophelia Overdose

Latex costume: Photo by Jamari Lior, Model: Ophelia Overdose

Latex costume: Photo by Phillip Ganzer, Model: Ophelia Overdose

Miss Overdose

ROYALBLACK

Model: Ophelia Overdose

Royal Black

LENA QUIST

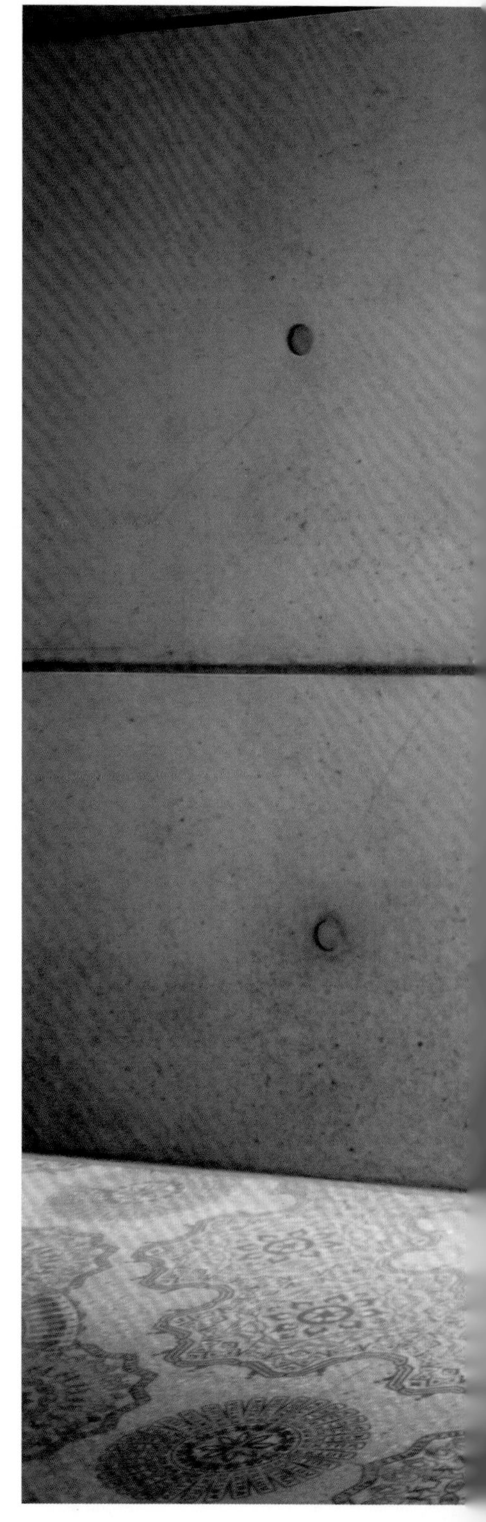

Lena Quist

TWOTWENTYTWO CLOTHING

TwoTwentyTwo Clothing

ELECTRIC IBIZA

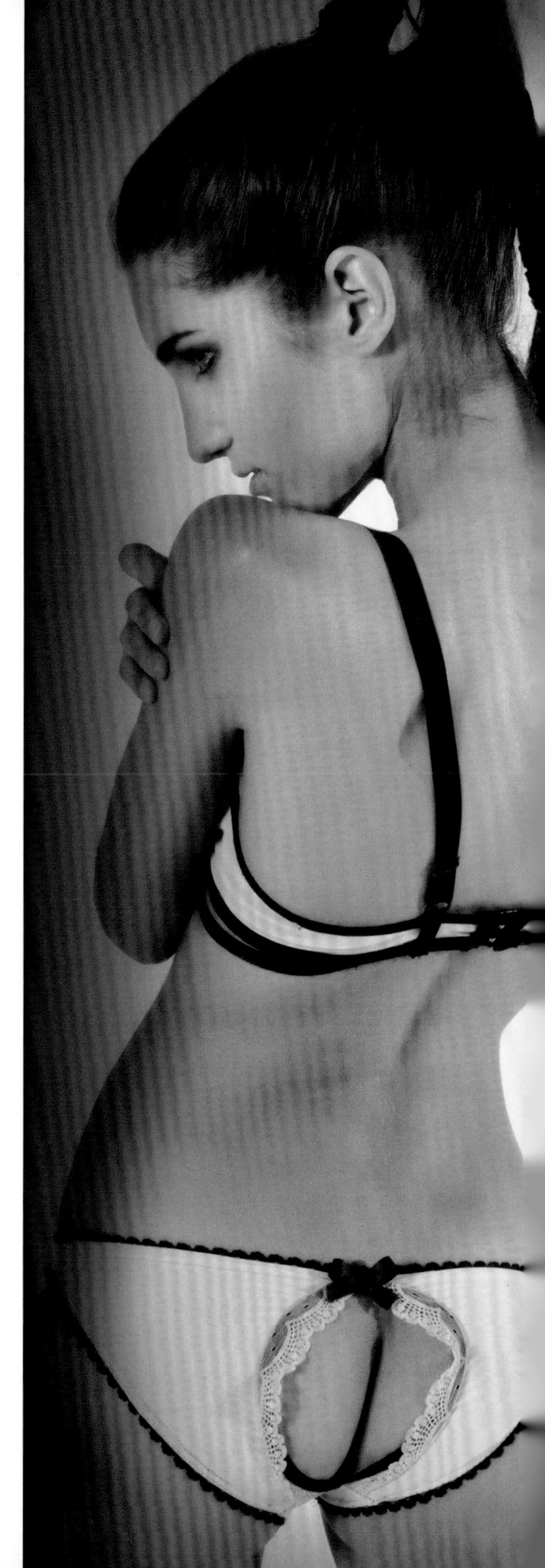

Electric Ibiza

FEISTY CAT

Feisty Cat

SHHH!
COUTURE

This too shall pass.

Shhh!

TATJANA WARNECKE
COSMIC COUTURE BERLIN

love

Model: Ophelia Overdose

Models: Miss Blutpuppe (left) & Ophelia Overdose

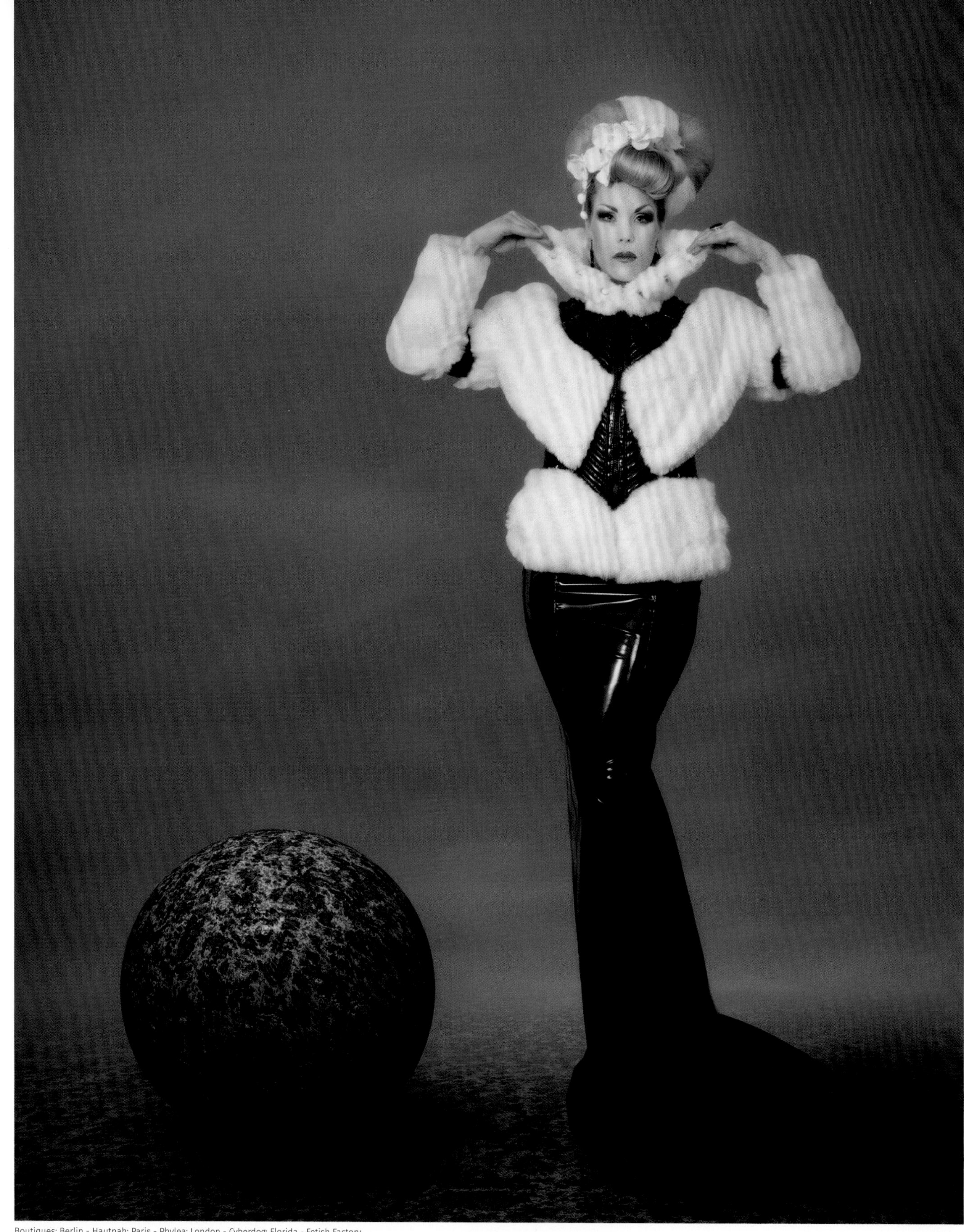

Boutiques: Berlin - Hautnah; Paris - Phylea; London - Cyberdog; Florida - Fetish Factory

Tatjana Warnecke

AM STATIK

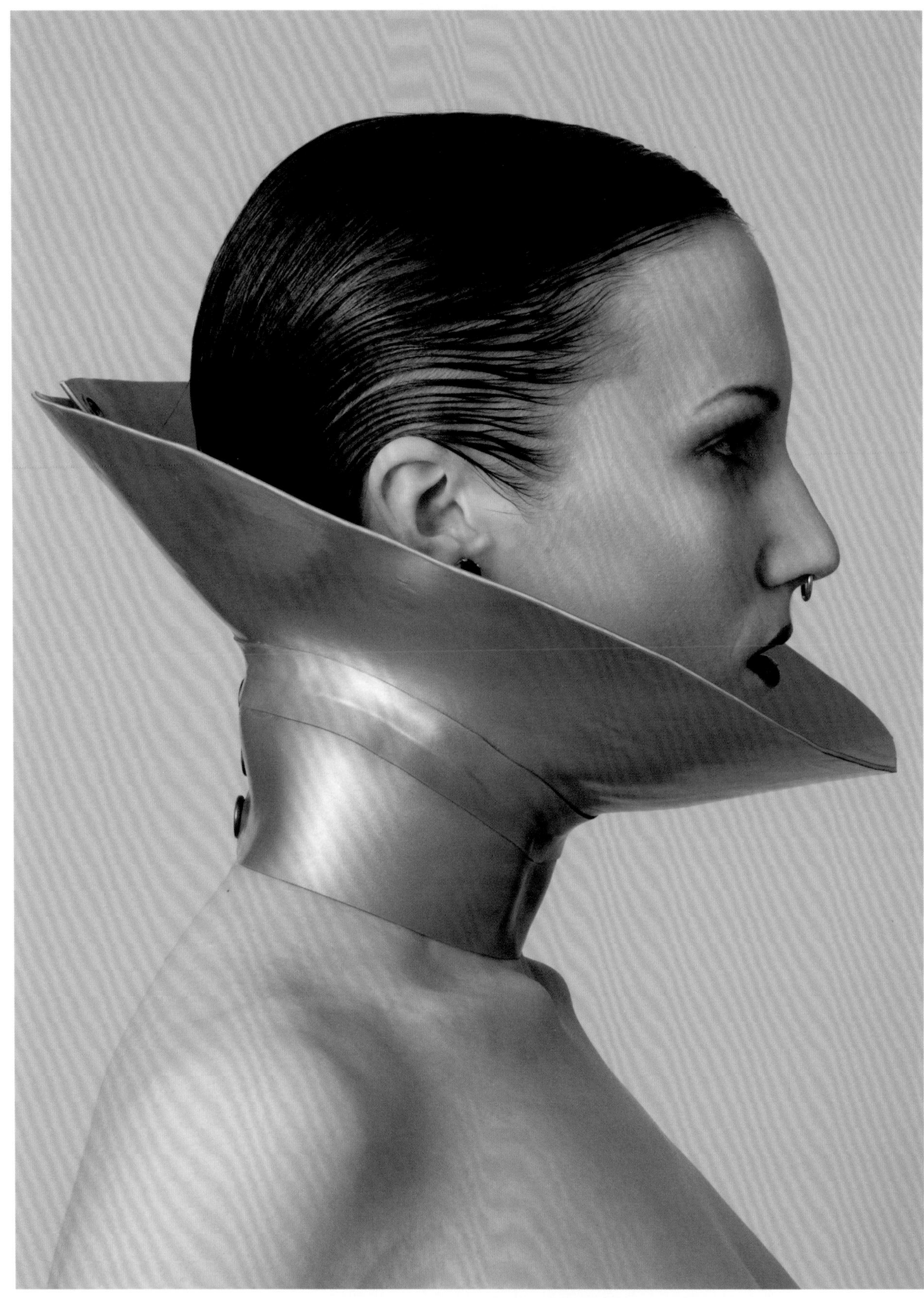

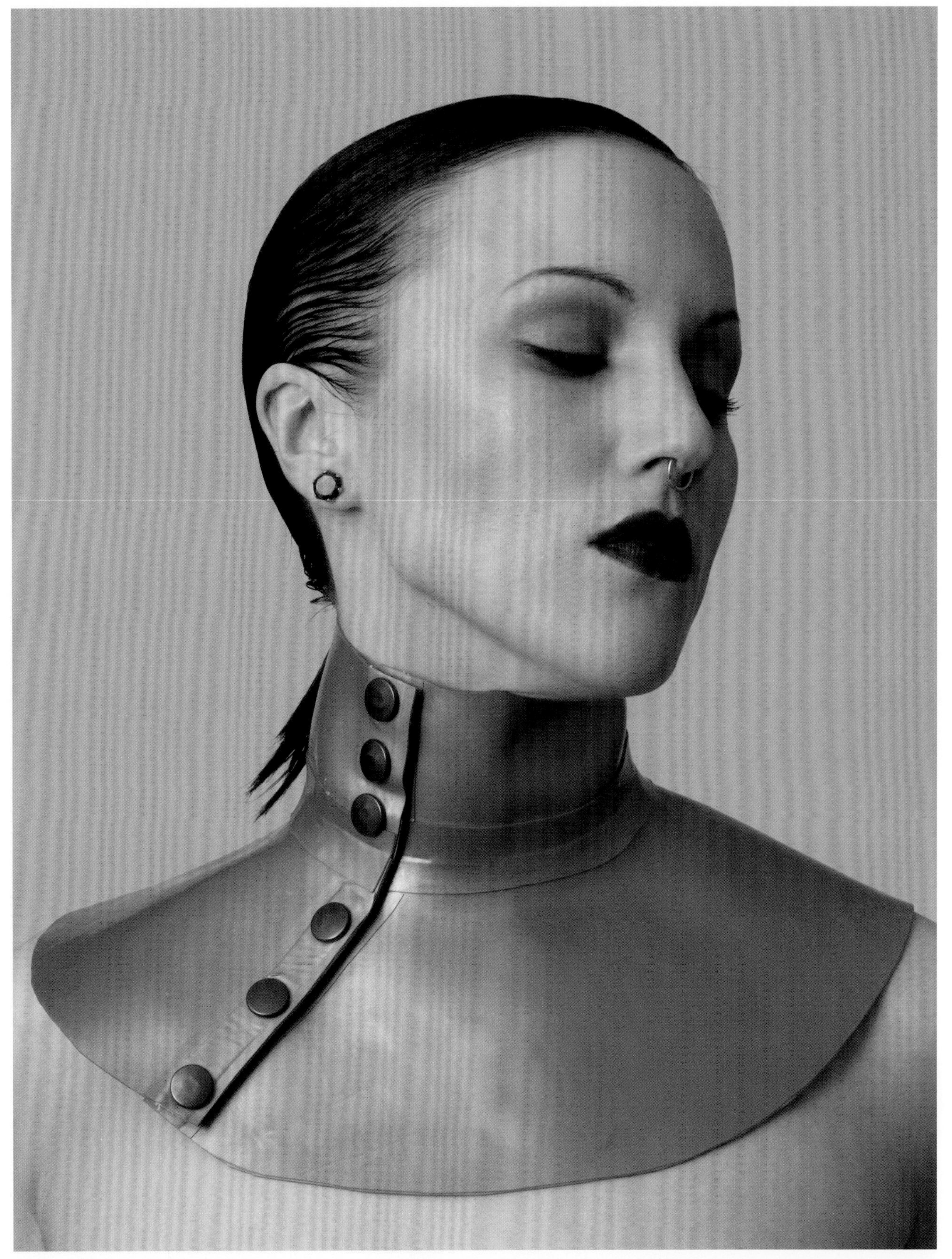

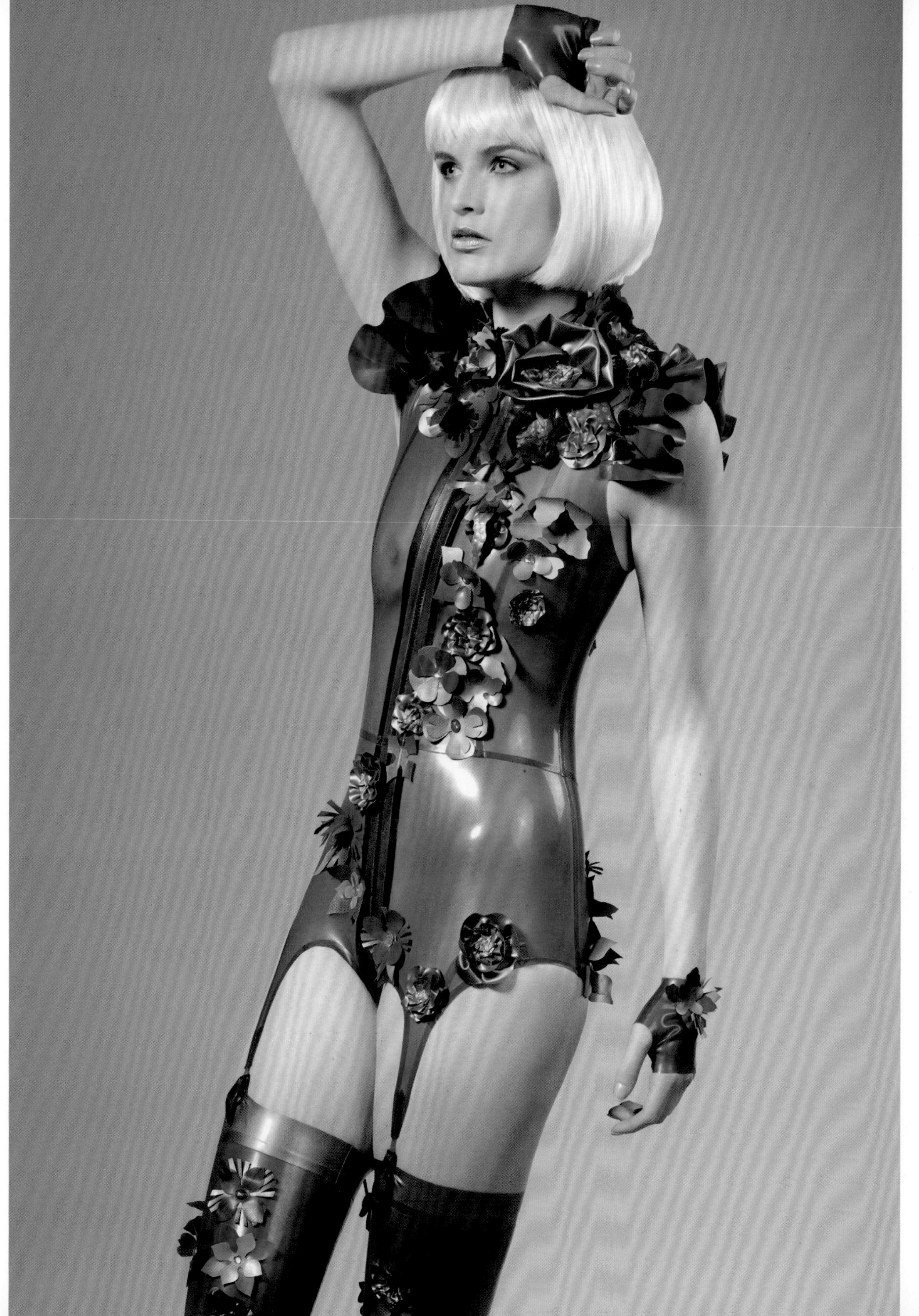

Am Statik

LIBIDEX LTD

Mendoza

Mendoza

Mendoza
ZENITH

Mendoza

Mendoza

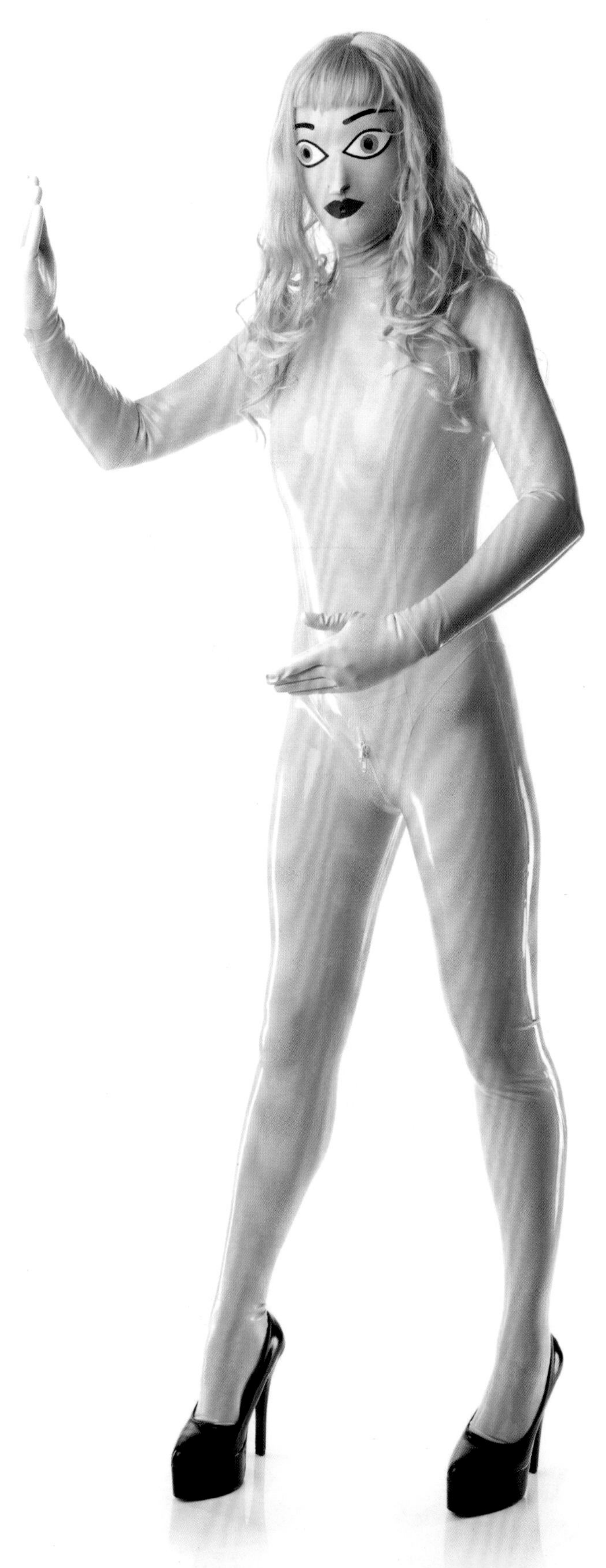

Libidex Ltd

FAVOR

Heineken
Havana Club

Heineken
eken
Spiegelau
Havana Club
El Ron de Cuba

favor

RALF FRANZ FOTODESIGN

HW Design

SENSUAL LATEX

FABULOUSLY LATEX

DONALD PILON

Donald Pilon

ARCANUM ACCESSORIES

Arcanum Accessories

CATHOUSE CLOTHING

Cathouse Clothing

ZITRONENRÖLLCHEN

Einspänner
3,20

Bombs over Betty

zitronenröllchen

KIMBERLICIOUS LATEX

Kimberlicious Latex

MAD DUCK DESIGNS

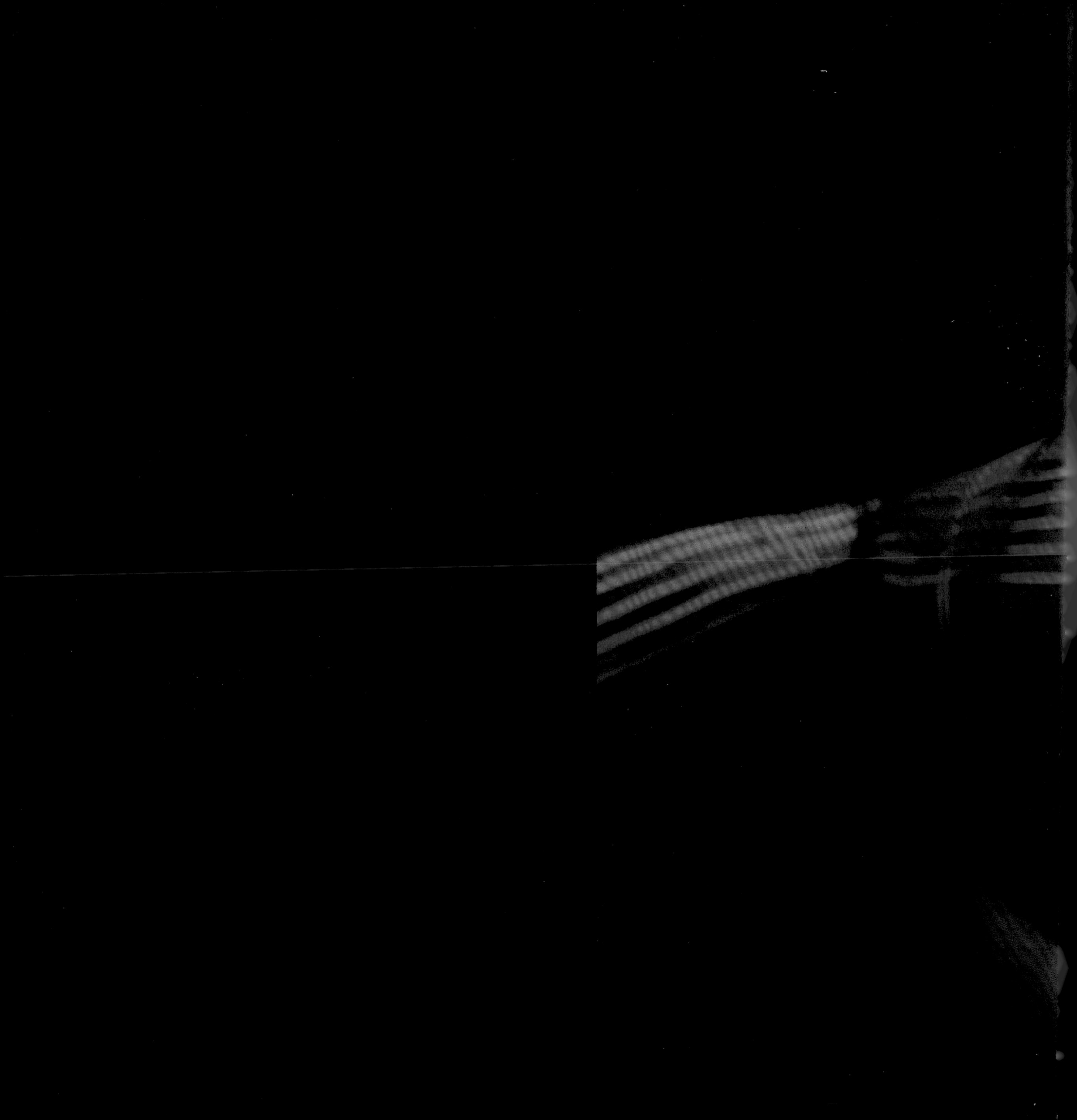

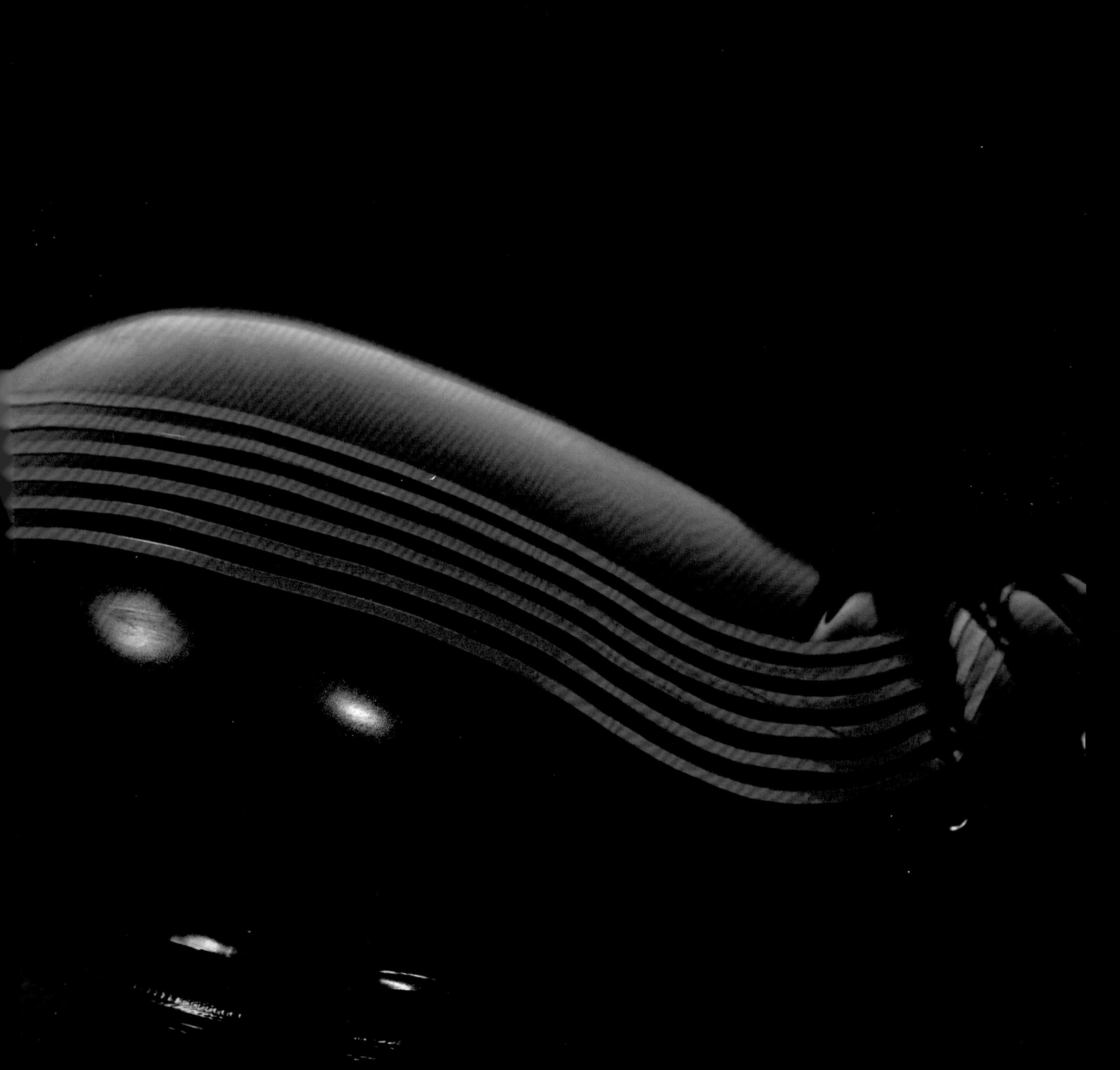

HOGE SPANNING
LEVENSGEVAARLIJK

gorenje

VALERIA ORLANDO

Valeria Orlando

TABLEAUX VIVANTS

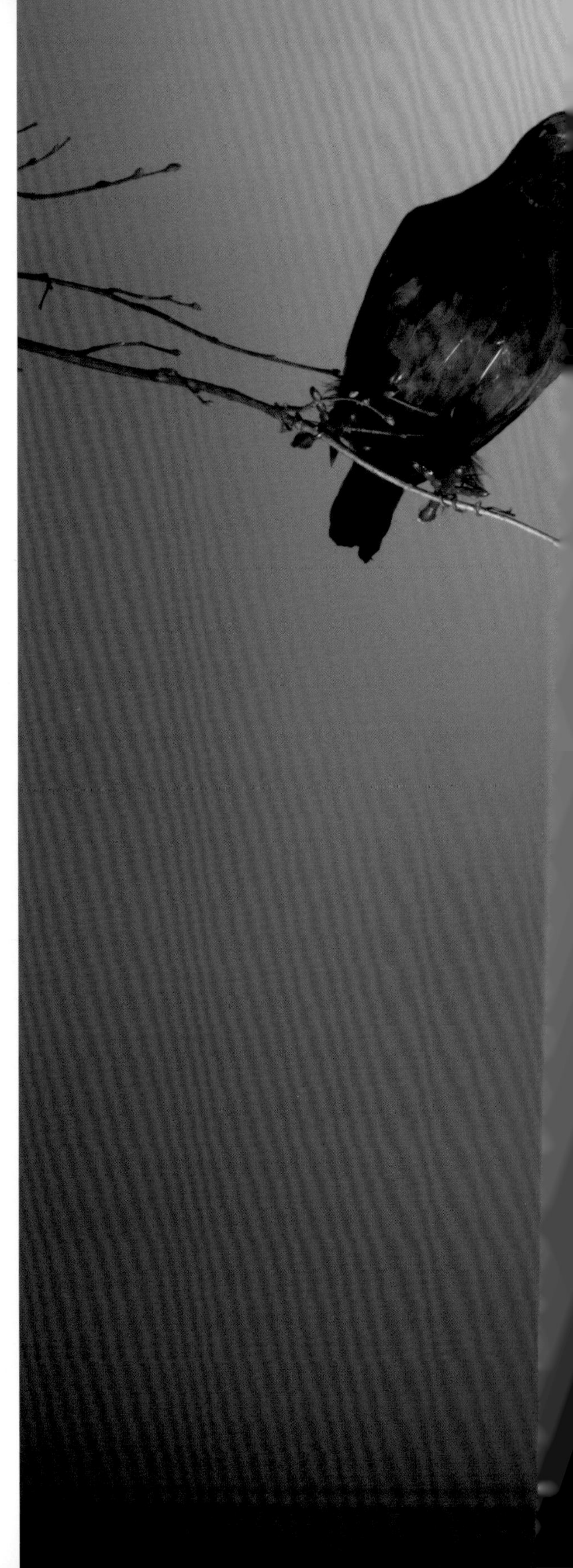

Bad

Bad
Bad

Tableaux Vivants

Photo credits

p 6 - 7 Ardita Fetish Fashion
© Thomas Bommi Burggraf
Model: Tifa Leone

p 8 - 9 Ardita Fetish Fashion
© Hartmut Nörenberg
Model: Ophelia Overdose

p 10 - 11
Ardita Fetish Fashion
© Stefan Gesell
Model: Ophelia Overdose

p 11 Ardita Fetish Fashion
© Massimo van der Leeuw
Model: Lotte Groeneweg

p 12 - 13 Ardita Fetish Fashion
© Massimo van der Leeuw
Model: Ellen Vogel

p 4 - 5; 14 -15; 16-17
Ardita Fetish Fashion
© Massimo van der Leeuw
Model: Rachael Vee

p 18 – 19; 24-27
Ardita Fetish Fashion
© Massimo van der Leeuw
Model: Ardita

p 20 - 21
Ardita Fetish Fashion
© Massimo van der Leeuw
Model: Megan Renee & Holly Santos

p 22 Ardita Fetish Fashion
© Massimo van der Leeuw
Model: Amelia Dinmore

p 23 Ardita Fetish Fashion
© Massimo van der Leeuw
Model: Lara Aimee

p 28 Collective Chaos
© Collective Chaos
Model: Kat Kalashnikov

p 29; 32 Collective Chaos
© Collective Chaos
Model: Courtney Crave

p 30 - 31; 38 – 39
Collective Chaos
© Collective Chaos
Model: Mosh

p 32 Collective Chaos
© Collective Chaos
Model: Miss Crash

p 33; Collective Chaos
© Collective Chaos
Model: Vaunt

p 34 - 35 Collective Chaos
© Collective Chaos
Model: Aliona

p 34 Collective Chaos
© Collective Chaos
Model: Theresa Manchester

p 35 Collective Chaos
© Collective Chaos
Model: Marlo Marquise

p 33, 40 - 41 Collective Chaos
© Collective Chaos
Model: Kess M

p 42 - 43 Collective Chaos
© Collective Chaos
Model: Ancilla Tilia

p 44 - 45 Collective Chaos
© Collective Chaos
Model: Sharon TK
p 46- 55 Lucky Dame
© Marta F. Andrés
Model: Steph Westwood

p 57 Westward Bound
© PhotoVance
Model: Jade Vixen

p 58 Westward Bound
© Marcus Gunnarsson
Model: Sister Sinister

p 59; 64 - 65; 72 - 73; 76
Westward Bound
© Moritz Maibaum
Model: Ophelia Overdose

p 60 Westward Bound
© Frank Sanders
Model: Haro

p 61 Westward Bound
© Miss Studio-X
Model: Jade Vixen

p 62 Westward Bound
© Gerhard Haan
Model: Lizzy Meow

p 63 Westward Bound
© Robert Gilbert
Model: Jasmine Virginia

p 66 Westward Bound
© Josefine Jönsson
Model: Tea Time

p 67 - 68 Westward Bound
© Oliver Kniest
Model: Sister Sinister

p 69 Westward Bound
© Jörg Hohmann
Model: Onna Sakura

p 70 - 73 Westward Bound
© Joseph O'Brien
Model: Ophelia Overdose

p 74; 77 - 79 Westward Bound
© Stefan Grosjean
Model: Ophelia Overdose

p 75 Westward Bound
© Marcus Gloger
Model: Onna Sakura

p 81 Rose Conway Photography
© Rose Conway
Designer: Westward Bound
Model: Juchi

p 82 - 84 Rose Conway Photography
© Rose Conway
Designer: Eustratia
Model: Millie Dollar

p 85 Rose Conway Photography
© Rose Conway
Designer: Westward Bound
Model: Acid Doll

p 86 Rose Conway Photography
© Rose Conway
Designer: Anatomic Bomb
Model: Helene Atsuko

p 87 Rose Conway Photography
© Rose Conway
Designer: Burning Violet Latex
Model: Millie Dollar

p 88 - 89 Rose Conway Photography
© Rose Conway
Designer: Westward Bound
Model: Melissa Hayward

p 90 - 91 Rose Conway Photography
© Rose Conway
Designer: Kaori's Latex Dreams
Model: Juchi

p 92 - 94 Rose Conway Photography
© Rose Conway
Designer: Ooh La Latex
Model: Ulorin Vex

p 95 Rose Conway Photography
© Rose Conway
Designer: Shhh! Couture
Model: Amie Conradine Gibson

p 96 - 97 Rose Conway Photography
© Rose Conway
Designer: Kaori's Latex Dreams
Model: Becky Burton

p 98 - 105 Heveas Heaven
© Sabrina Rynas

p 106 - 113 Inner Sanctum
© Sabrina Rynas

p 114 - 119 Showroom Inner Sanctum/ Heveas Heaven
© Sabrina Rynas

p 120 Maebelle Latex
© Josefine Jönsson
Model: Lillithy

p 121 Maebelle Latex
© Josefine Jönsson
Model: Starfucked

p 122 - 123 Maebelle Latex
© Josefine Jönsson
Model: Arathin

p 124 Maebelle Latex
© Josefine Jönsson
Model: Navalith

p 125 Maebelle Latex
© Josefine Jönsson
Model: Insanitea

p 126 - 127 Maebelle Latex
© Josefine Jönsson
Model: Varga Frostnatt

p 128 - 129 Lovely Latex
© Stefan Gesell
Model: Ophelia Overdose

p 132 Lovely Latex
© Phoebusphoto
Model: Marie Kalista

p 133 Lovely Latex
© Cojac Photography
Model: Milla Vie & Marie Kalista

p 134 - 135 Lovely Latex
© Cojac Photography
Model: Mark

p 136 - 137 Lovely Latex
© Thomas Burggraf
Model: Rachael V

p 138 - 149 dos santos
© Marcel Steeger

p 151; 154 - 163 Eustratia
© Jennifer Byron
Model: Biomechanina

p 156 Eustratia
© Julian M Kilsby
Model: Ryo (left)

p 164 - 165 Cyberesque
© silent-view
Models: Swantje & Nika & Miss Cyberesque

p 166 Cyberesque
© silent-view
Model: Miss Cyberesque

p 167 Cyberesque
© silent-view
Model: Nika

p 168 - 169 Cyberesque
© silent-view
Models: Swantje & Lisa Vandalism

p 170 Cyberesque
© silent-view
Model: Lisa Vandalism

p 171 Cyberesque
© silent-view
Models: Swantje & Lisa Vandalism & Nika & Miss Cyberesque

p 172 Cyberesque
© Alex Blyg
Model: Ophelia Overdose

p 173 Cyberesque
© Gili Shani
Model: Sinteque

p 174 Cyberesque
© Gili Shani
Models: Minerva & Lilith

p 175 Cyberesque
© Gili Shani
Model: Lilith

p 176 Cyberesque
© Gili Shani
Model: Gabor; Tominous

p 177 Cyberesque
© Gili Shani
Model: Minerva

p 179 Blacklickorish Latex
© Alejandra Guerrero
Model: Marlo Marquise

p 180 - 181 Blacklickorish Latex
© Maxime Avet
Model: Ancilla Tilia

p 182 Blacklickorish Latex
© Ezra Spurrier
Model: Abandoned Building

p 183 Blacklickorish Latex
© Mobius Prime
Model: Vivka

p 184 - 185 Blacklickorish Latex
© Graphics Metropolis
Models: Minerva Mendez & Olivia Price

p 186 - 187 Blacklickorish Latex
© Allan Amato
Model: Skin Diamond

p 188 Blacklickorish Latex
© Allan Amato
Model: Stoya

p 189 Blacklickorish Latex
© Allan Amato
Models: Velocity & Ulorin Vex

p 190 Blacklickorish Latex
© Christine Kessler
Model: Darenzia

p 191 Blacklickorish Latex
© Allan Amato
Model: Ulorin Vex

p 192 Blacklickorish Latex
© Angela Marklew
Model: Olga Chaplinskaya

p 192 Blacklickorish Latex
© Insobel De Lisle
Model: Elegy Ellem (left top)

p 192 Blacklickorish Latex
© Allan Amato
Model: Mosh (left middle)

p 192 Blacklickorish Latex
© Allan Amato
Model: Ruby True (left bottom)

p 193 Blacklickorish Latex
© Allan Amato
Model: Zoetica Ebb

p 194 - 199 Godfrey Knight Designs
© John Chilton
Design by Richard Knight
Made by Zahira's Boudoir

p 200 - 201; 202 - 203; 205
ainsley-t shoes
© Giordano Affolti

p 204; 206; 207 ainsley-t shoes
© Andrea Zani

p 208 - 209; 210 - 211
ainsley-t shoes
© Sarah McGlathery

p 212 - 216 Gore Couture & Creations by Liv Free
© ASYLUMseventy7
Model: Imogen Sotos-Castello

p 216 - 217 Gore Couture
© BJA Visuals
Model: Razor Candi

p 218 - 219 Gore Couture
© BJA Visuals
Models: Eden Prosper & Razor Candi

p 222 Miss Overdose
© Moritz Maibaum
Model: Ophelia Overdose

p 223 Miss Overdose
© Marcus Gunnarsson
Model: Elegy Ellem; Ophelia Overdose

p 224 - 225 Miss Overdose
© Moritz Maibaum
Model: Ophelia Overdose

p 226 - 227 Miss Overdose
© Hartmut Nörenberg
Model: Ophelia Overdose

p 228 Miss Overdose
© Jamari Lior
Model: Ophelia Overdose

p 229 Miss Overdose
© Phillip Ganzer
Model: Ophelia Overdose

p 230 - 231 Royal Black
© Doris Karlovits
Model: Frauke Voigas

p 232 Royal Black
© Heiner Seemann / Grauton
Model: La Esmeralda

p 233; 235 Royal Black
© Morgana
Model: Morgana

p 234 Royal Black
© Hartmut Nörenberg
Model: Ophelia Overdose

p 235 Royal Black
© Doris Karlovits
Model: Katia Wagner

p 236 Royal Black
© Alex Blyg
Model: La Esmeralda

p 238 - 239 Royal Black
© Verena Mandragora
Model: Maja Siegmund

p 238 - 239 Royal Black
© Verena Mandragora
Model: Maja Siegmund; Anna Ullrich

p 240 - 243 Lena Quist
© Markus Kinnunen
Model: Helena Björnström
Styling: Lena Quist

p 244 Lena Quist
© Markus Kinnunen
Model: Helena Björnström

p 245 Lena Quist
© Markus Kinnunen
Model: Johanna Öman

p 246 - 247 Lena Quist
© Amanda Stiverius
Model: Emma Lundahl

p 250 - 251 Lena Quist
© Oliver Wong
Model: Kiara Ferraro

p 252 - 253 Lena Quist
© Markus Kinnunen
Model: Harriet Arnberg

p 254 - 255 TwoTwentyTwo Clothing
© Warn Photography
Model: Sarah Marie Hilker

p 256 - 257 TwoTwentyTwo Clothing
© Warn Photography
Model: Shayla Beesley

p 258 - 259 TwoTwentyTwo Clothing
© Warn Photography
Model: Emily Lazar

p 260 - 265 TwoTwentyTwo Clothing
© Jessica Flavin Photography
Model: Precious Little; V Nixie; Amanda Darling
Airbrush artist: Julian Weiss

p 266 - 269 Electric Ibiza
© Ben Swyre
Model: Lucie Reckovasa

p 270 - 271; 272 - 273 Feisty Cat
© www.feisty-cat.com
Model: Sinteque

p 274 Feisty Cat
© Feisty Cat
Model: Jana WildAtHeart

p 275 Feisty Cat
© Feisty Cat
Model: Frau Pepper

p 276 Feisty Cat
© www.feisty-cat.com
Model: Valentina DeMonia

p 278 - 279 Feisty Cat
© Feisty Cat
Model: Haydee Sparks

p 280 - 281 Feisty Cat
© Feisty Cat
Model: Clea Cutthroat

p 286 - 287; 289 Latex – Shhh! Couture Handmade Latex
© Julian M Kilsby
Model: Ruby True

p 288 Latex – Shhh! Couture Handmade Latex
© Julian M Kilsby
Model: Cervená Fox

p 290 Latex – Shhh! Couture Handmade Latex
© Hatter Marie
Model: Miss Mischief

p 291 Latex – Shhh! Couture Handmade Latex
© Sean Chasney
Model: Vicky Christina

p 292 Latex – Shhh! Couture Handmade Latex
© Toxic Imaging

p 293 Latex – Shhh! Couture Handmade Latex
© Gary Stevens
Model: Kimber Lee

p 294 Latex – Shhh! Couture Handmade Latex
© Julian M Kilsby
Model: Cervená Fox

p 295 Latex – Shhh! Couture Handmade Latex
© J. Isobel de Lisle
Model: Elegy Ellem

p 296 - 297 Latex – Shhh! Couture Handmade Latex
© Sean Chasney
Model: Vicky Christina

p 298 - 299; 307 Tatjana Warnecke – Cosmic Couture Berlin
© Ronan Budec
Model: Anastasia

p 300 Tatjana Warnecke – Cosmic Couture Berlin
© Alex Blyg
Model: La Esmeralda

p 301- 302 Tatjana Warnecke – Cosmic Couture Berlin
© Alex Blyg
Model: Lady Alexa

p 303 Tatjana Warnecke – Cosmic Couture Berlin
© Pictureart Gallery
Model: Xarah von den Vielenregen

p 304 Tatjana Warnecke – Cosmic Couture Berlin
© Achim Webel
Model: Dragon

p 305 Tatjana Warnecke – Cosmic Couture Berlin
© Alex Blyg –
Model: Eric

p 308 Tatjana Warnecke – Cosmic Couture Berlin
© Seelenphotographie
Model: Lady Alexa

p 310 Tatjana Warnecke – Cosmic Couture Berlin
© Jamari Lior
Model: Ophelia Overdose

p 311 Tatjana Warnecke – Cosmic Couture Berlin
© Jamari Lior
Model left: Miss Blutpuppe
Model right: Ophelia Overdose

p 315 Am Statik
© Justine Louise
Model: Becky Burton

p 316 Am Statik
© Kris Talikowski
Models: Aerynn & Sohui

p 317 Am Statik
© Kris Talikowski
Model: Charly Ridley

p 318 - 319 Am Statik
© Amy Day
Model: Angelica Thistel

p 320 - 321 Am Statik
© Amy Day
Model: Ruby True

p 322 - 323 Am Statik
© Justine Louise
Model: Becky Burton

p 324 - 325 Am Statik
© Kris Talikowski
Model: Sohui

p 328 - 333 Libidex Ltd
© Terry Mendoza

p 334 - 342 Libidex Ltd
© Gothic Image

p 344 - 345, 348 - 249; 354 - 355 favor
© Benedikt Ernst
Model: Indigo International

p 346 - 347, 350 - 351, 353 favor
© Benedikt Ernst
Model: Sharon Moe

p 348, 355 favor
© Ralf König
Model: Indigo International

p 352 favor
© Benedikt Ernst
Model: Dae Joon

p 356 - 363 Ralf Franz Fotodesign
© Ralf Franz

p 364 - 365 HW Design
© Berserker
Model: Sinteque

p 366 HW Design
© Harald Wilfer
Model: Kumi Monster

p 367 HW Design
© Harald Wilfer
Model: Anna Vorski & Sandra

p 368 HW Design
© Harald Wilfer
Model: Rebecca & Sandra

p 369 HW Design
© Stephan Doleschal
Models: Tina & Dante Posh

p 371 HW Design
© Eric Martin
Model: Kumi Monster

p 372 - 375, 376 - 377 Sensual Latex
© Andi Bell, Rebell Arts
Model: Zora

p 378 Sensual Latex
© Andi Bell, Rebell Arts
Model: Juliane Bischoff

p 379 Sensual Latex
© M.A. Wottawa
Model: MiriMa

p 380 Sensual Latex
© Andi Bell, Rebell Arts
Model: Lumina

p 381 Sensual Latex
© RM Photodesign
Model: Lumina

p 382 Sensual Latex
© RM Photodesign
Model: Chrissi

p 383 Sensual Latex
© Martin Petermann
Model: Aranea Peel

p 384 - 385, 386 - 387 Sensual Latex
© PicAss Foto
Model: LuziLu

p 388 - 395 Fabulously Fetish
© Elis Berg
Model: Miss Mosh

p 396 - 399 Fabulously Fetish
© Steve Prue
Model: Miss Miranda

p 400 - 401 Donald Pilon
© Donald Pilon
Model: Donal Pilon

p 402 - 403 Donald Pilon
© Donald Pilon
Model: Patrick Fabian

p 404 - 405, 406 - 411 Arcanum Accessories
© Miss Rain
Model: Anna Fur Laxis

p 412 - 413 Arcanum Accessories
© Jazz 'Hans' Photography
Model: Anna Fur Laxis

p 414 - 423 Cathouse Clothing
© James Alexander Photography

p 425 zitronenröllchen
© JeyOh!
Model: Victoria van Violence

p 426 zitronenröllchen
© Bombs over Betty
Models: Masuimi Max & Megan Renee (right)

p 427 zitronenröllchen
© Aerynn
Model: Elegy Ellem

p 430 zitronenröllchen
© roqueFIVEphoto
Model: Kris

p 431 zitronenröllchen
© roqueFIVEphoto
Models: Kris & Lee

p 432 zitronenröllchen
© roqueFIVEphoto
Models: Lee

p 434 - 435 zitronenröllchen
© Isaac Suttell
Model: Erika Tschirhart

p 436 - 437 Kimberlicious Latex
© Shannon Brooke Imagery
Model: Megan Renee

p 438 Kimberlicious Latex
© Scott R Kline
Model: Megan Renee

p 439; 440 - 441 Kimberlicious Latex
© A. Grey
Model: Kataxena

p 442 - 443 Kimberlicious Latex
© ATP Studios
Model: Megan Renee

p 444 - 445 Kimberlicious Latex
© Ceri Davies
Model: Hazel Jones

p 446 mad duck designs
© Robert Pichler
Model: Lizzy Meow

p 447 - 449 mad duck designs
© Werner Hrabak

p 450 - 454 mad duck designs
© Fräulein C photographic artwork
Model: Miss Mad

p 462 - 464 Valeria Orlando Makeup & Hair
© Eolo Perfido Photography

p 466 - 467 Tableaux Vivants
© Elle Muliarchyk (Management Artists Organization)
Model: Lucie Von Alten (IMG)

p 468 - 469 Tableaux Vivants
© Elle Muliarchyk (Management Artists Organization)
Model: Tonya (IMG)

p 470 - 473 Tableaux Vivants
© Jahn Hall
Model: Morthyn Roc

p 474 - 475 Tableaux Vivants
© Elle Muliarchyk (Management Artists Organization)
Model: Lucie Von Alten (IMG)

p 476 Tableaux Vivants
© Elle Muliarchyk (Management Artists Organization)

p 477 Tableaux Vivants
© Elle Muliarchyk (Management Artists Organization)
Model: Lucie Von Alten (IMG)

KÖNEMANN

www.koenemann.com

6, rue du Mail – 75002 Paris
www.victoires.com
Dépôt légal : 2e trimestre 2019
ISBN 978-2-8099-1607-2

Editor: Michelle Schmidt
Layout/imaging/pre-press: Finn Göpfert (elrebel)

Printed in China by Shenzhen Hua Xin Colour-printing & Platemaking Co., Ltd

ISBN 978-3-7419-2154-4